Grams
Teaches
Kyliee
The Importants of
Prayer

BREN DANIELS

GRAMS TEACHES KYLIEE THE IMPORTANTS OF PRAYER

iUniverse books may be ordered through booksellers or by contacting:

iUniverse
1663 Liberty Drive
Bloomington, IN 47403
www.iuniverse.com
844-349-9409

ISBN: 978-1-6632-2076-9 (sc)
ISBN: 978-1-6632-2165-0 (hc)
ISBN: 978-1-6632-2077-6 (e)

Print information available on the last page.

iUniverse rev. date: 04/26/2021

PRAYER
IS
IMPORTANT

I dedicate this Book to Kyliee Hamilton. At a very young age she would always watch what I do. When she would come visit me or stay over at my house for the weekend. She would notice how long I pray. How long I study. She would even tell me I take too long. She would notice me praying to God. And even when she saw me praying. If her mom would say what is your Grams doing if I was in another room? When she saw me praying. She would say she talking to God. I know she is very special. And she has learned the important of prayer at a young age. I love my Kyliee.

$\mathcal{I}$ntroduction

This Book is written about my first granddaughter Kyliee at the age of 3 years old up to the age of 5 years old. I began to teach her about prayer. And to let her know it's very important to spend time in prayer talking to God. Because he do answer prayer.

Matthew 19:14 But Jesus said, suffer little children, and forbid them not, to come unto me; for of such is the kingdom of heaven.

Hi my name is Kyliee and my Grams teaches me the important of prayer.

My Grams would take me to Church.

Bren Daniels

Grams taking
Kyliee to Church

My Grams would take me to school sometimes, she would pray for me before I get out the car.

Bren Daniels

Grams praying
for Kyliee
before dropping
her off at
School

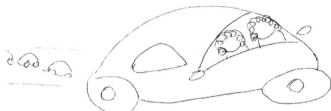

I would see my Grams praying.

Bren Daniels

When I see my Grams praying at night.

I asked her to pray for my mom.

Kylee sees
Grams praying
at night

When I would see my Grams praying.

She would tell me to be quiet.

My sister and I was over one morning at Grams house.

And she was praying.

Grams told us we have to be quiet.

She said we have to respect prayer.

My sister and
I watching
Grams pray

Bren Daniels

Sometimes when I see my Grams praying.

I would tell her she takes too long.

Then she would say.

You can't put a time on how long you pray.

Kyliee telling
Grams she takes
to long while
praying

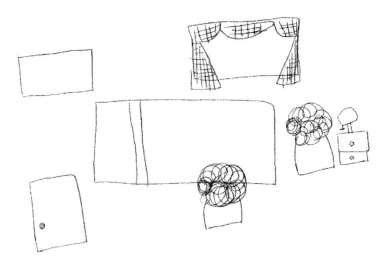

My mom and sister and I.

We went to see my Grams one day.

And while we were at her house in her bedroom.

I asked my Grams to pray for someone?

I was only 3 years old.

Kyliee asking
Grams to pray
for someone

I asked my Grams to pray for someone I wanted to see.

My Grams and mom was surprised I asked.

My Grams teaches me to thank God for the food before eating.

Bren Daniels

Grams teaches
Kyliee to thank
God before
eating her
food

One day my Grams came to pick me up from the after school daycare.

When Grams picked me up riding home in the back seat.

I said Grams did you pray?

Bren Daniels

It's still the same.

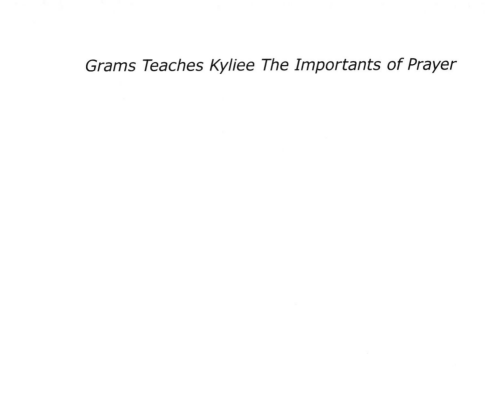

Grams was shocked I said that.

Bren Daniels

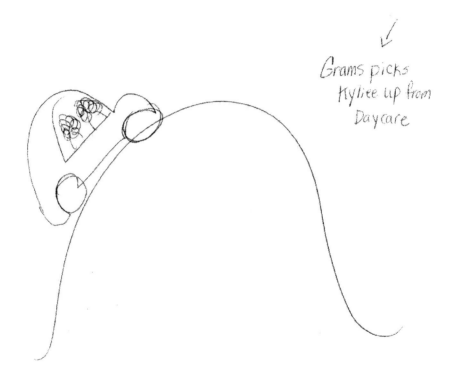

Grams picks
Kylice up from
Daycare

My mom and I stayed over by my Grams one night.

The next day my mom asked me what was my Grams doing in her room?

I said talking to God.

My mom said that girl.

She laughed at what I said.

I saw my Grams praying.

My Grams started teaching me how to pray.

My Grams would give me the words to say.

I would say Father God In The Name of Jesus.

Thank you LORD for my mama.

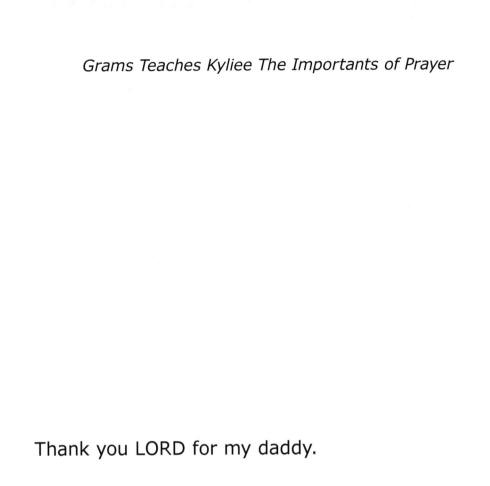

Thank you LORD for my daddy.

Thank you LORD for my sister.

Thank you LORD for my cousins.

Thank you LORD for my Grams.

Thank you LORD for my Aunt.

Thank you LORD for my family.

Then my Grams started teaching me the Our Father prayer.

Matthew 6:9-13

Our Father which art in heaven,

Hallowed be thy name.

Thy kingdom come.

Bren Daniels

Thy will be done in earth,

as it is in heaven.

Bren Daniels

Give us this day our daily bread.

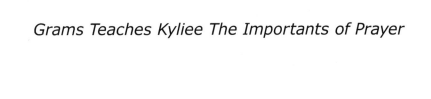

And forgive us our debts,

as we forgive our debtors.

And lead us not into temptation,

Bren Daniels

but deliver us from evil:

For thine is the kingdom,

Bren Daniels

and the power,

and the glory,

Bren Daniels

for ever

A-men.

My mom and sister and I stayed over at my Grams house another time.

The next morning I went in the room were my Grams was and she was studying her Bible.

Later on I came back in her room she was still studying.

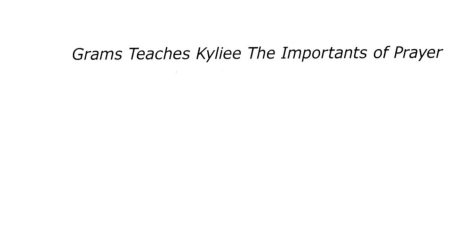

Grams studies for hours.

Bren Daniels

I told Grams you take too long.

Grams says you can't put a time on how long you study.

Grams tell me you have to be quiet while I am studying.

Kyliee tells Grams
she takes to long
while she studies
her Bible

Bren Daniels

Grams takes me to school another time.

Immediately when she stops the car.

I said Grams you didn't pray for me.

Grams said I didn't forget.

I had to stop the car first.

Grams laughed at me.

I was use to my Grams praying for me.

When she drops me off at school.

Bren Daniels

Kylice thinks
Grams forgot to
Pray for her.

When Grams comes over to my house.

Before leaving sometimes she would pray for me.

So I asked Grams to pray for my sister?

Kyliee wants
Grams to pray
for her sister

When my Grams and I was praying.

I wanted to pray for some things I wanted.

I would say it while I was praying.

What I wanted.

Kyliee praying
asking for some
things she wants
from God

Because I was praying.

My Grams brought me a bike.

Grams buys Kylee
a bike. She
said because I
was praying,
God told her to buy
me a bike

When I went by my neighbor house one day.

I took my I-Pad.

And I put it on gospel music.

A song my Grams always listen too.

They told me you got that from your grandmother.

Kylice goes by
neighbor house
listening to gospel
music on her
I-Pad

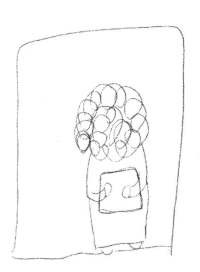

I started to love to pray.

I would ask my Grams could I pray.

One day I told my Grams to teach my mom how to pray.

She said I already did.

That's why she has a Book about her,

that I have already written.

A Little Girl Name Destiny Who Loves to Pray.

My mom has her own book about her.

Because she loved to pray.

I would ask my Grams could I go to Church with her.

I love to go to Church with my Grams.

I would say today is Saturday.

Because I knew after Saturday was Sunday.

That was the day we go to Church.

I would go to Church a lot with my Grams.

I like to pick my own clothes out for Church.

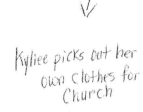

Kyliee picks out her own clothes for Church

Sometimes when I go to Church with Grams.

Sometimes she would go up and sing.

And I would say you going to sing?

I like to see my Grams sing at Church.

I be sitting there clapping my hands.

Kyliee watching
Grams sing at
Church

Grams would take me to get prayer,

in the prayer line at Church.

So that I could do good at school.

We would stand in line.

Grams takes me
up to get prayer
at Church

When Grams taught me how to pray.

I would want to do it all by myself.

Without Grams helping me.

Kyliee wanting to
Pray all by herself
Without Grams
helping

When I go to Grams house sometimes.

I see Grams watching preaching on T.V.

So one day I came over.

I asked to listen to the Pastor she always listening too?

Grams and I
watching preaching
on T.V.

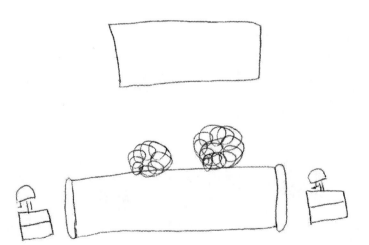

Bren Daniels

When I am riding in Grams car.

She always playing her gospel c-d's.

It's one person I always like to hear.

When I am riding in Grams car.

I asked Grams who she were?

I would ask Grams to play that song?

Kyliee asked Grams to play a song in the car

Grams came by my house one night.

And I was getting ready for bed.

I told Grams I wanted to pray.

Grams was so glad to hear me say that.

She said that's so sweet.

And she hugged me.

Kyliee telling
Grams she wants
to pray

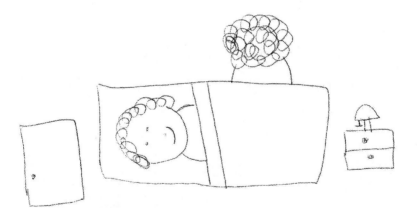

I went to Church with my Grams.

And the Pastor was praying for people standing in line.

I asked my Grams could I go get prayer?

And would she go up there with me.

My Grams was surprised that I asked her.

My Grams said come on.

I will go with you.

I was at the age of 5 years old.

Kyliee asked Grams to take her up to get prayer

Sometimes my Grams would want my mom to see how, she has been working with me.

Teaching me how to pray.

She would have me to pray in front of my mom.

Bren Daniels

Kyliee praying
in front of
mom and Grams

Helpful Hints To Parents And Grandparents

1. When you teach them about prayer. And they began to know the important of prayer. They will want to pray.

2. So teach your children how to pray. And Grams teach your grand children how to pray.

3. Grandparents you can take them to Church sometimes.

4. Children watch what you do.

5. Just like she would ask me could she pray. But if I had never been working with her teaching her how to pray. She could not have asked me.

6. There have been times she would pray for me. I would let her.

7. I would tell her to pray for her mom and sister. And her family and friends.

8. She would want to listen to gospel music. Because she seen me doing it.

9. She would tell me to put certain people on my c-d in my car. And in my house on T.V. Because she hear them in my car all the time. And she always see them on my T.V. when she comes to my house.

10. I would tell her to say her grace before eating to give God thanks.

11. I would teach her to pray for her mom, sister, brother, those that are apart of her life.

To God Be All The Glory, Honor and Praise for every Book I write.

I cannot write without being Inspired by the Holy Ghost.

That is why all the Glory Belongs to God for every Book I write.

I am just elated that he chose me to write for him.

For I know nothing without him. My hand is a pen of a ready writer.

Thank you Jesus

By: Bren Daniels
Jesus The Writer